MY MORTIFIED LIFE

MY MORTIFIED LIFE

A Guided Journal to Gauge How Much
You've Changed Since Childhood

Dave Nadelberg
with Sam Kaplan

For Carolyn, whose love of diaries was the first of many reasons we loved her.

Published in the United States by
Ulysses Press
P.O. Box 3440
Berkeley, CA 94703
www.ulyssespress.com

ISBN: 978-1-64604-166-4
Library of Congress Control Number: 2017938176

Printed in the United States
10 9 8 7 6 5 4 3 2 1

Acquisitions editor: Keith Riegert
Managing editor: Claire Chun
Editor: Alice Riegert
Proofreader: Shayna Keyles
Design, layout, and illustrations: Katie Tonkovich
Cover photos: printed with permission from Julia Wright, Sakena Patterson, Laurent Martini, and Glenda Graves
Interior photography from Shutterstock.com, page 5 (boombox) © Ivan Bondarenko; page 35 (car) © John Lloyd; page 55 (phone) © totojang1977; pages 88–89 (cassette) © Ensuper; page 109 (Ouija board) © fjimenezmeca; page 128 (computer) © artsplav; page 147 (legs) © Awe Inspiring Images; pages 177 (globe) © Glyphstock; pages 194–95 (mirror) © Megapixel; page 213 (beer bottle) © immfocusstudio

My childhood self dedicates the following journal to

_____.

My adult self dedicates the following journal to

_____.

Table of Contents

Why We Made This Journal

How much have you changed since childhood?
Are you still the same introvert? Extrovert? Go-getter?
Bed-wetter? Warrior? Wimp? Nightmare? Neat freak?

For over fifteen years, we've been asking questions like this in *Mortified*—an international storytelling project (on stage, page, screen, radio, internet) that celebrates the angst and awkwardness of growing up. With this book, our debut diary, we're tackling the relationship between past and present, head-on.

Behold, a guided journal for your two selves: your awkward inner child and your (equally awkward) inner adult. Part journal, part time machine, this is a diary for people who never kept one as kids, and also for people who've been addicted to them their whole lives. Our goal? To create a fun tool for self-reflection.

How to Use This Journal

 Answer a question about your childhood on pages marked "THEN." Choose any age (0–18) to write about. We leave that up to you.

 Answer the same question about your adulthood on pages marked "NOW."

 Rate how much you believe you've changed using the "Change-O-Meter" found at the bottom of each entry. Are you the same? Are you different? The results may surprise (or mortify) you.

 At the end of the book, average all your ratings to see just how much you've actually changed over the years. Is this a totally scientific experiment? Yes, absolutely. 100 percent. There is no disputing it.

Score-tified!

Using the scale below, predict what score you'll average by the end of this book. When you complete the journal, check back and see how you fared.

Are you a creature of habit? Proof that good things never change—like Betty White? Or are you an agent of change? Proof that transformation is awesome—like David Bowie?

ARE YOU A BETTY OR A BOWIE?
CIRCLE WHERE YOU FALL ON THE SPECTRUM BELOW

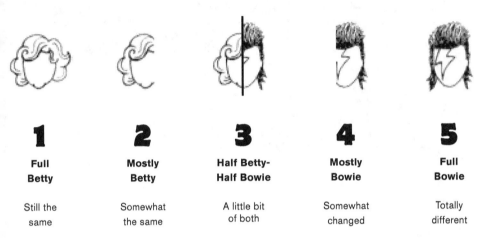

1	2	3	4	5
Full Betty	**Mostly Betty**	**Half Betty-Half Bowie**	**Mostly Bowie**	**Full Bowie**
Still the same	Somewhat the same	A little bit of both	Somewhat changed	Totally different

Tips for Getting the Most from This Journal

- Resist judgments. This is an activity to encourage self-reflection, not superiority or shame. Your degree of change is neither good nor bad. Change does not inherently make someone more evolved. Likewise, consistency does not make someone more authentic.

- Look past the surface. Push yourself to discover how much each Then/Now answer actually has in common. Likewise, push yourself to see how much each answer differs.

- Pick an age. When writing about your past, we leave it up to you to choose which part of childhood (grade school, early teens, late teens) to journal about. Pick the age that resonates most for you.

- Interpret each prompt however you want. Our goal is to inspire you to reflect on your past and present by exploring them side by side. We included a bunch of optional follow-up questions to stimulate your brain. They're merely food for thought, as there's not room to answer all.

- Share with your BFF. Do this with friends and compare your final results.

Chapter One

My Mortified Heart

MY DUMB HEART

What's the dumbest romantic blunder you ever committed— or someone committed while pursuing you?

Why was it so dumb? What was the outcome? Did other people hear about it?
How did you feel about it? What did you learn from it?

MY DUMB HEART

What's the dumbest romantic blunder you committed this year—or someone committed while pursuing you?

Why was it so dumb? What was the outcome? Did other people hear about it?
How did you feel about it? What did you learn from it?

CRUSHING IT

Who was your first BIG crush growing up?

Describe their personality, style, and looks. Why were you attracted to them?
Did they know your name? Did you ever do anything about it? Why? How'd it go?

♥

CRUSHING IT

Who is your biggest crush today? And yes, celebrities count too!

Describe their personality, style, and looks. Why are you attracted to them?
Do they know your name? Did you make a move? Why? How'd it go?

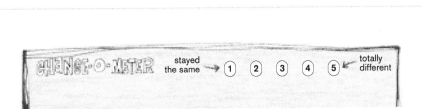

SHOOTING BLANKS

As a teenager . . .

I thought about sex: _____ times a day.

I got off: _____ times a week.

Sex was more important than: _____.

The weirdest tool I ever used to masturbate was: _____.

When I masturbated, it took: _____ seconds/minutes/hours to finish.

The weirdest place I ever masturbated was: _____.

The weirdest thing I ever masturbated to/with was: _____.

My go-to aid for masturbation was: _____.

My biggest turn-ons were: _____.

When I hooked up, I usually lasted: _____ seconds/minutes/hours.

SHOOTING BLANKS

As an adult . . .

I think about sex: _____ times a day.

I get off: _____ times a week.

Sex is more important than: _____.

The weirdest tool I've used to masturbate was: _____.

When I masturbate, it takes: _____ seconds/minutes/hours to finish.

The weirdest place I've masturbated was: _____.

The weirdest thing I ever masturbated to/with was: _____.

My go-to aid for masturbation is: _____.

My biggest turn-ons are: _____.

When I hook up, I usually last: _____ seconds/minutes/hours.

RELATIONSHIPS

Describe your top three romantic relationships growing up.

What were their first names? Any cutesy nicknames? What did you like most about each?
What did you dislike most? How long did each relationship last? How did each
end? (If you didn't have three, interpret "relationship" however you want.)

1

2

3

RELATIONSHIPS

Describe your top three romantic relationships as an adult.

What are their first names? Any cutesy nicknames? What did you like most about each?
What did you dislike most? How long did each relationship last? How did each
end? (If you didn't have three, interpret "relationship" however you want.)

DATE NIGHT

What do you remember most about your first date growing up?

Who was it with? Where did you go? Were you nervous? What'd you talk about?
What was the best part? Worst part? How did it end? (And yes, group dates totally count.)

DATE NIGHT

What's your biggest memory of your most recent date?

Who was it with? Where did you go? Were you nervous? What'd you talk about?
What was the best part? Worst part? How did it end? (And yes, group dates totally count.)

CHANGE-O-METER   stayed → (1) (2) (3) (4) (5) ← totally
the same   different

HEARTBREAKER

Take a time machine back to your very first heartbreak—who broke your heart and how?

Why did it happen? How bad did it hurt? What was your relationship like before the heartbreak? How did you cope? Did you ever get over it and how?

EXTRA CREDIT

Breaking Up Is Hard

What's the most memorable breakup excuse you ever gave, or someone gave to you, growing up?

HEARTBREAKER

Think back to your most recent heartbreak— who broke your heart and how?

Why did it happen? How bad did it hurt? What was your relationship like before the heartbreak? How did you cope? Have you gotten over it? How?

Breaking Up Is Hard

What's the most memorable breakup excuse you ever gave, or someone gave to you, as an adult?

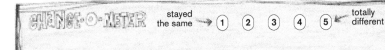

| | stayed the same → | 1 | 2 | 3 | 4 | 5 | ← totally different |

17

DRAW YOUR PERFECT MATCH

Imagine you're in high school and you stumble upon a magical device that lets you design your ideal love. Did that person exist in real life or are they a unicorn? Draw a diagram of your perfect mate and their accessories.

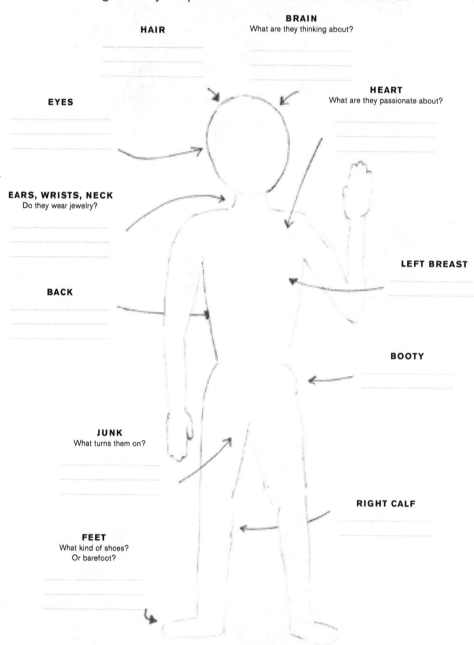

HAIR

BRAIN
What are they thinking about?

EYES

HEART
What are they passionate about?

EARS, WRISTS, NECK
Do they wear jewelry?

LEFT BREAST

BACK

BOOTY

JUNK
What turns them on?

RIGHT CALF

FEET
What kind of shoes?
Or barefoot?

DRAW YOUR PERFECT MATCH

You just stumbled upon a magical device that lets you design your
ideal love. Does this person exist in real life or are they a unicorn?
Draw a diagram of your perfect mate and their accessories.

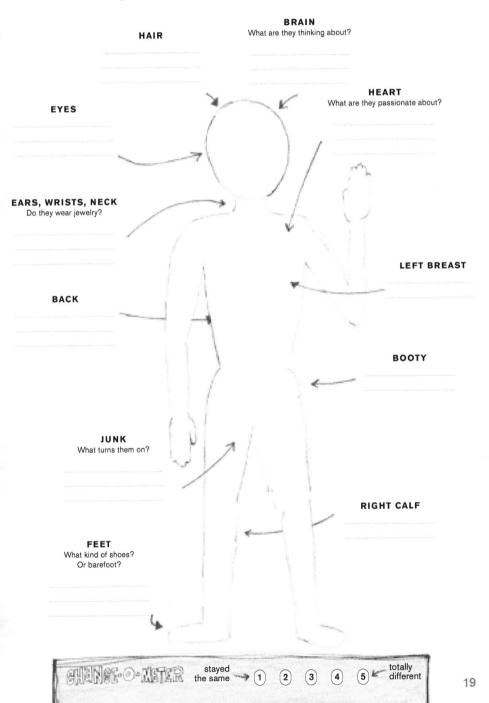

BRAIN
What are they thinking about?

HAIR

HEART
What are they passionate about?

EYES

EARS, WRISTS, NECK
Do they wear jewelry?

LEFT BREAST

BACK

BOOTY

JUNK
What turns them on?

RIGHT CALF

FEET
What kind of shoes?
Or barefoot?

CHANGE-O-METER   stayed the same → ① ② ③ ④ ⑤ ← totally different

SEXUAL ENCOUNTERS OF THE NERD KIND

Describe your first . . .

Kiss. Who was it with? Where was it? What was the build up? How did it feel?

_____

_____

_____

_____

_____

Hookup. Who was it with? Where was it? What was the build up? How did it feel?

_____

_____

_____

_____

_____

Home run. Who was it with? Where was it? What was the build up? How did it feel?

_____

_____

_____

_____

_____

SEXUAL ENCOUNTERS OF THE NERD KIND

Describe your most recent . . .

Kiss. Who was it with? Where was it? What was the build up? How did it feel?

Hookup. Who was it with? Where was it? What was the build up? How did it feel?

Home run. Who was it with? Where was it? What was the build up? How did it feel?

 CHANGE-O-METER stayed the same → ① ② ③ ④ ⑤ ⬅ totally different   21

MY WILD SIDE

In high school . . .

My most embarrassing sexual encounter was

My best sexual encounter was:

My worst sexual encounter was:

My kinkiest sexual encounter was:

My riskiest sexual encounter was:

MY MORTIFIED LIFE

MY WILD SIDE

In the last five years . . .

My most embarrassing sexual encounter was

My best sexual encounter was:

My worst sexual encounter was:

My kinkiest sexual encounter was:

My riskiest sexual encounter was:

CHANGE-O-METER stayed the same → ① ② ③ ④ ⑤ ← totally different

AWW, THANKS SWEETHEART!

What was the sweetest romantic gesture you've ever done—or that was ever done for you—growing up?

What made it so memorable? What did it teach you?

♥

AWW, THANKS SWEETHEART!

What was the absolute sweetest romantic gesture you did—or that was done for you—in the past year?

What made it so memorable? What did it teach you?

 stayed the same → ① ② ③ ④ ⑤   totally different

SEXUAL INSECURITIES

What was your biggest sexual insecurity as a teenager?

Why? Where did that insecurity stem from? How much of this fear was due to
actually being teased versus how much of it was in your head? How did this
insecurity change your behavior: what you ate, wore, did, revealed?

SEXUAL INSECURITIES

What is your biggest sexual insecurity these days?

Why? Where does that insecurity stem from? How much of this fear is due to actually being teased versus how much of it is in your head? How does this insecurity change your behavior: what you eat, wear, do, reveal?

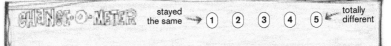

PEACOCKING

As a teen, did you act differently around somebody you liked, and how?

Which parts of your personality did you exaggerate? What parts of yourself did you hide or minimize? Did you lie or embellish anything about yourself? Was this "romantic persona" effective or not? Did you like being that other version of yourself?

PEACOCKING

Do you still act differently around people you like today, and how?

Which parts of your personality do you exaggerate? What parts of yourself do you
hide or minimize? Do you lie or embellish anything about yourself? Is this "romantic
persona" effective or not? Do you like being that other version of yourself?

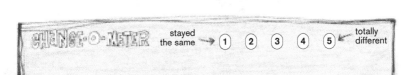

stayed the same → ① ② ③ ④ ⑤ ← totally different

♥

DON'T BE CRUEL

Growing up, what was the cruelest thing you
did to someone in the name of love?

_____

_____

_____

_____

_____

_____

_____

_____

_____

_____

What was the cruelest thing someone did to you in the name of love?

_____

_____

_____

_____

_____

_____

_____

_____

DON'T BE CRUEL

As an adult, what's the cruelest thing you've done to someone in the name of love?

What was the cruelest thing someone did to you in the name of love?

CHAPTER SUMMARY

Congratulations! You finished this chapter.

Now comes the fun part—figure out how much you've changed. Are you proof that good things always stay the same, like Betty White? Or are you proof of the power of transformation, like David Bowie?

CALCULATE YOUR SCORE!

Total all your Change-O-Meter scores from this chapter

The number of questions in this chapter

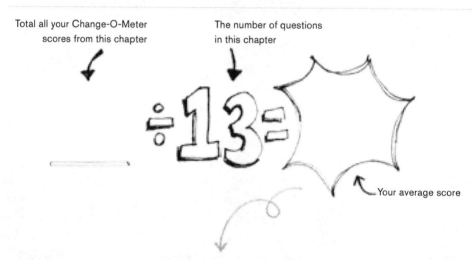

Your average score

ARE YOU A BETTY OR A BOWIE?
CIRCLE WHERE YOU FALL ON THE SPECTRUM BELOW

1	**2**	**3**	**4**	**5**
Full Betty	**Mostly Betty**	**Half Betty- Half Bowie**	**Mostly Bowie**	**Full Bowie**
Still the same	Somewhat the same	A little bit of both	Somewhat changed	Totally different

What parts of your love life have changed the least? Did that surprise you?

What parts of your love life have changed the most? Did that surprise you?

What questions were the hardest to answer in this chapter and why?

Was it harder to answer about your childhood or adulthood for this chapter?

What judgments do you have, if any, on the ways you have (and have not) changed?

Do any of these results inspire you to want to change some aspect of your life? If so, what?

Chapter Two

My
Mortified
Family

DRAW YOUR FAMILY

Using color (and preferably crayons, for safety), draw a scene depicting your family growing up, however you defined your family.

This drawing should capture the essence of how you felt about your family. How close were you? Did you do fun stuff? Awful stuff? Were you happy or angry when you were together? Were you closer to certain family members?

DRAW YOUR FAMILY

Using color (and preferably a pen, for maturity), draw a scene depicting your current family, however you define your family.

This drawing should capture the essence of how you feel about your family.
How close are you? Do you do fun stuff? Awful stuff? Are you content or furious
when you're together? Are you closer to certain family members?

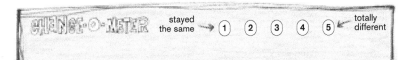

MEET THE PARENTS

Let's get real: when you were in high school, you had strong feelings towards your parents. Write down three things you loved and hated most about your parents.

(And yes, we know "hate" is a strong word, but this is a journal. If you can't get your strongest feelings out here, where can you express them?)

PARENT ONE

Name: _____ Relationship: _____

Describe the 3 things you LOVE most about this parent	Describe the 3 things you HATE most about this parent

PARENT TWO

Name: _____ Relationship: _____

Describe the 3 things you LOVE most about this parent	Describe the 3 things you HATE most about this parent

MEET THE PARENTS

Let's keep getting real: you have strong feelings towards your current family. Choose two family members who mean a lot to you (mom, dad, wife, husband, son, daughter, etc.) and write down the three things you love and hate most about them.

FAMILY MEMBER ONE

Name: _____ Relationship: _____

Describe the 3 things you LOVE most about this family member	Describe the 3 things you HATE most about this family member

FAMILY MEMBER TWO

Name: _____ Relationship: _____

Describe the 3 things you LOVE most about this family member	Describe the 3 things you HATE most about this family member

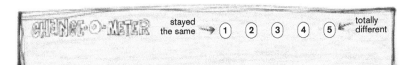

stayed the same ➡ ① ② ③ ④ ⑤ ← totally different

PARENTS JUST DON'T UNDERSTAND

Take a time machine back to the worst fight you ever had with your parent(s) growing up.

What caused that fight? Who was more at fault? What were the worst things said?
How did the fight change the relationship? Did you make up?

PARENTS JUST DON'T UNDERSTAND

Take a smaller time machine back to the worst fight you had with your parent(s) in the past five years.

What caused that fight? Who was more at fault? What were the worst things said?
How did the fight change the relationship? Did you make up?

CHANGE-O-METER   stayed the same → ① ② ③ ④ ⑤ ← totally different   41

MY MORTIFIED SIBLINGS

List your siblings, if any. How did you feel about each, growing up?*

Did you get along? Could you confide in them? Did they protect you? Were you the oldest, youngest, or were you a middle child? How do you think your birth order affected your personality?

> * If you are an only child, describe how you felt (and still feel) about not having siblings. Did you wish you had them—then and now? Was there anybody in your life that played a "sibling" role—then and now? How was/is this relationship different from others? Did/do you have imaginary friends?

MY MORTIFIED SIBLINGS

List your siblings, if any. How do you feel about each, today?*

Do you get along? Can you confide in them? What parts of your life do you share
with them? How do you think your birth order affects your personality?

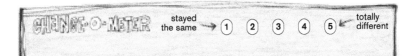

YAY! FAMILY IS AWESOME!

What was the single best family day you had growing up?

How old were you? Who was there? What did you do? What made the day so perfect (or close to perfect)? What specific memories stand out from that day?

YAY! FAMILY IS AWESOME!

What was the best family day you had in the past few years?

Who was there? What did you do? What made the day so perfect (or close to perfect)?
What specific memories stand out from that day?

45

HOUSEHOLD COMMANDMENTS

What were the most important rules in your household growing up?

Curfew, no cursing, always brush your teeth before bed, eat your broccoli or forfeit dessert, etc.

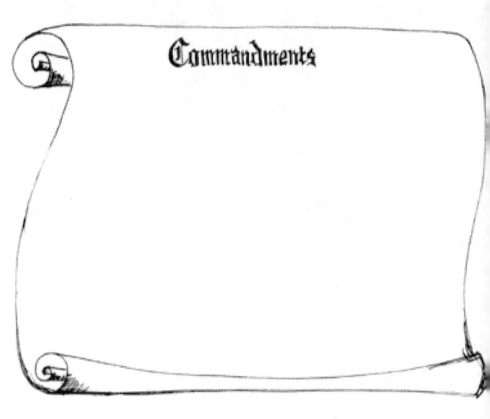

Commandments

Now pick one rule—how did you feel about it?

Was it fair? Did you follow it? Whine about it? Secretly resent it? Why?

HOUSEHOLD COMMANDMENTS

What are the most important rules in your current household?

If you're a parent: write the rules you've made for your children. If you live with roommates: write the "household rules." If you're living with a romantic partner: what are the things they nag you about (or you nag them about)? If you're living by yourself, what rules have you made for yourself? If you still live with your parents, see previous page.

Commandments

Now pick one rule—how do you feel about the rules?

Is it fair? Do you (or your housemates/partner/children) follow it? Whine about it? Secretly resent it? Why?

CHANGE-O-METER stayed the same → ① ② ③ ④ ⑤ ← totally different

47

YOU'RE GROUNDED, YOUNG LADY!

Describe the most severe punishments you received growing up.

1 Transgression:

Punishment:

Was the punishment warranted?

2 Transgression:

Punishment:

Was the punishment warranted?

3 Transgression:

Punishment:

Was the punishment warranted?

YOU'RE GROUNDED, YOUNG LADY!

If you're a parent, what are the biggest punishments you've doled out to your children?

(If you don't have children, how do you think your current self would discipline your teenage self for the transgressions described on the previous page?)

1. Transgression:

Punishment:

Was the punishment warranted?

2. Transgression:

Punishment:

Was the punishment warranted?

3. Transgression:

Punishment:

Was the punishment warranted?

CHANGE-O-METER   stayed the same → ① ② ③ ④ ⑤ ← totally different

49

MOMMY DEAREST

Great news! You've discovered a special machine that lets you send one letter back in time, but you can only send it to one family member.

Choose the family member and then send the letter.

Dear _____,

MOMMY DEAREST

Great news: pens and paper still exist, which means you can still send letters!

Choose one family member to send an actual handwritten letter or postcard to via snail mail. Like, actually do this. We mean it. Write a letter and send it. (You can use this page to pen a draft or record a copy of the letter you end up sending.)

Dear _____,

CHAPTER SUMMARY

Congratulations! You finished this chapter.

Now comes the fun part—figure out how much you've changed. Are you proof that good things always stay the same, like Betty White? Or are you proof of the power of transformation, like David Bowie?

CALCULATE YOUR SCORE!

Total all your Change-O-Meter scores from this chapter

The number of questions in this chapter

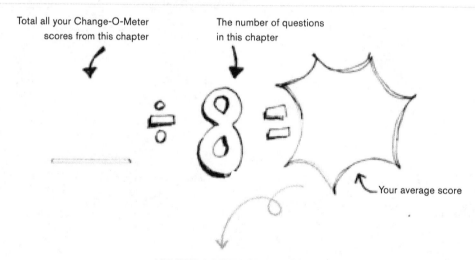

Your average score

ARE YOU A BETTY OR A BOWIE?
CIRCLE WHERE YOU FALL ON THE SPECTRUM BELOW

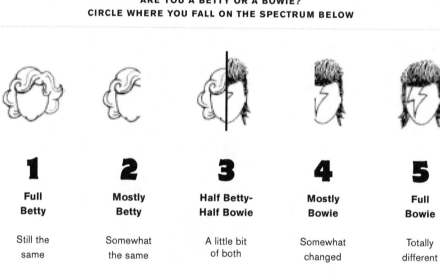

1	**2**	**3**	**4**	**5**
Full Betty	**Mostly Betty**	**Half Betty-Half Bowie**	**Mostly Bowie**	**Full Bowie**
Still the same	Somewhat the same	A little bit of both	Somewhat changed	Totally different

What parts of your family life or family identity have changed the least? Did that surprise you?

What parts of your family life or family identity have changed the most? Did that surprise you?

What questions were the hardest to answer in this chapter and why?

Was it harder to answer about your childhood or adulthood for this chapter?

What judgments do you have, if any, on the ways you have (and have not) changed?

Do any of these results inspire you to want to change some aspect of your life? If so, what?

CHAPTER THREE

MY MORTIFIED SOCIAL LIFE

BUT, LIKE DOES HE LIKE LIKE HER?

CLIQUES THAT STICK

What were the subcultures that you identified with, or wanted to identify with, growing up (i.e., goths, greasers, gamers, band geeks, hippies, skanks, skaters, juggalos, jocks, etc.)?

What attracted you to these subcultures? What did your parents think? What, if anything, did you change about yourself in order to be accepted into these subcultures?

CLIQUES THAT STICK

What are the subcultures that you identify with, or want to identify with, today (i.e., yuppie, foodie, yogi, liberal, conservative, queer, etc.)?

What attracts you to these subcultures? What do you currently think of the subcultures you were into as a teen? What, if anything, do you change about yourself in order to be accepted into these subcultures?

CLIMBING THE SOCIAL LADDER

What qualities—such as humor, popularity, common interests, loyalty—did you look for in friends when you were growing up?

Did you make friends who were super cool and popular? Or did you hang out with people who did their own thing? Were your friends loyal, or did they ever betray you in order to climb a rung on the social ladder?

Growing up, what kind of friend were you?

Why do you think your friends hung out with you? Because you were cool and popular, or because you did your own thing? Were you loyal to your friends, or did you ever betray anybody in order to climb a rung on the social ladder?

CLIMBING THE SOCIAL LADDER

What qualities—such as humor, success, common interests, loyalty—do you look for in friends these days?

Do you choose friends who are super successful? Or do you make friends with people because of their personality? Are your friends mostly good for a night of fun, or are they always there for you when you need them? How real can you get with them? Has your group of friends changed or stayed pretty much the same throughout adulthood?

Nowadays, what kind of friend are you?

Why do you think your friends hang out with you? What "role" do you play in your friendships? Have you changed friends or stuck by your buddies through thick and thin?

CHANGE-O-METER stayed the same → ① ② ③ ④ ⑤ ← totally different

MY BFFS

My best friend as a kid was: _____

What I liked most about them was:

When we hung out, we usually:

But our favorite thing to do together was:

My best friend in middle school was: _____

What I liked most about them was:

When we hung out, we usually:

But our favorite thing to do together was:

My best friend in high school was: _____

What I liked most about them was:

When we hung out, we usually:

But our favorite thing to do together was:

MY BFFS

My closest friend in my personal life is: _____

What I like most about them is:

When we hang out, we usually:

But our favorite thing to do together is:

My closest friend in my professional life is: _____

What I like most about them is:

When we hang out, we usually:

But our favorite thing to do together is:

My closest friend from a community or a club is: _____

What I like most about them is:

When we hang out, we usually:

But our favorite thing to do together is:

CHANGE-O-METER stayed the same → (1) (2) (3) (4) (5) ← totally different

KNOW THY ENEMY

My archenemy in elementary school was: _____

I hated them so much because: _____

_____

The worst thing they ever did to me was: _____

Whenever I saw them, I: _____

I dealt with my hatred by: _____

The worst moment of our feud was when: _____

My archenemy in middle school was: _____

I hated them so much because: _____

_____

The worst thing they ever did to me was: _____

Whenever I saw them, I: _____

I dealt with my hatred by: _____

The worst moment of our feud was when: _____

My archenemy in high school was: _____

I hated them so much because: _____

_____

The worst thing they ever did to me was: _____

Whenever I saw them, I: _____

I dealt with my hatred by: _____

The worst moment of our feud was when: _____

KNOW THY ENEMY

My archenemy in my personal life today is: _____

I hate them so much because:

The worst thing they ever did to me was:

Whenever I see them, I:

I deal with my disdain by:

The worst moment of our feud was when:

My archenemy in my professional life today is: _____

I hate them so much because:

The worst thing they ever did to me was:

Whenever I see them, I:

I deal with my disdain by:

The worst moment of our feud was when:

My archenemy in pop culture or politics who doesn't know my name, but damn, do I hate their stupid guts, is: _____

I hate them so much because:

The worst thing they ever did to me was:

Whenever I see them, I:

I deal with my disdain by:

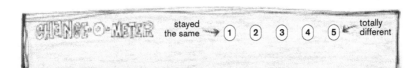

CHANGE-O-METER stayed the same → ① ② ③ ④ ⑤ ← totally different

MY SOCIAL SPHERE

Complete the "sociogram" about your high school relationships.

Instructions: Using the bubbles provided, write the names of the
people you had relationships with growing up.

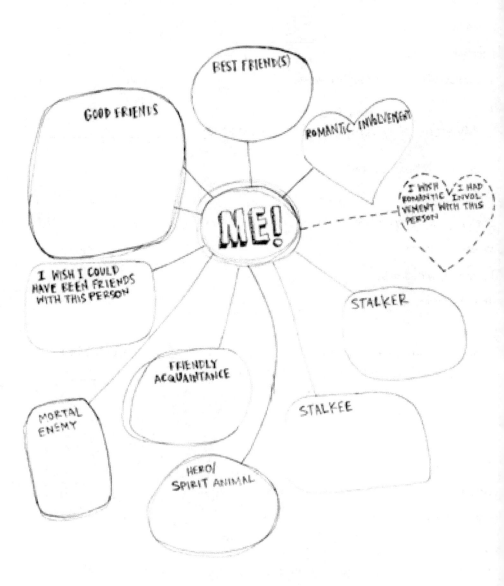

MY SOCIAL SPHERE

Complete the "sociogram" about your current social relationships.

Instructions: Using the bubbles provided, write the names of the
people you have relationships with these days.

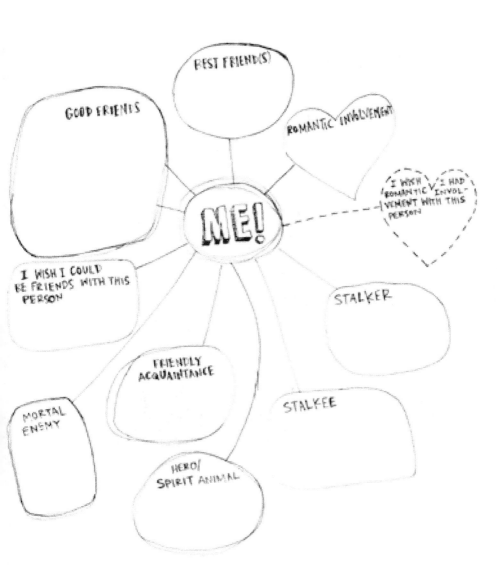

- BEST FRIEND(S)
- GOOD FRIENDS
- ROMANTIC INVOLVEMENT
- I WISH I HAD ROMANTIC INVOLVEMENT WITH THIS PERSON
- ME!
- I WISH I COULD BE FRIENDS WITH THIS PERSON
- STALKER
- MORTAL ENEMY
- FRIENDLY ACQUAINTANCE
- STALKEE
- HERO/ SPIRIT ANIMAL

CHANGE-O-METER   stayed the same → ① ② ③ ④ ⑤ ← totally different

PEOPLE SUCK

Which friend hurt you the most growing up, and what did they do?

Why did it sting so bad? Why do you think they did it? How did you respond?
Does it still hurt? Did you ever forgive them? Do you still let people like this into your
life? What did you learn from the pain? How do you think the pain changed you?

PEOPLE SUCK

Which friend hurt you the most as an adult, and what did they do?

Why did it sting so bad? Why do you think they did it? How did you respond?
Does it still hurt? Did you ever forgive them? Do you still let people like this into your
life? What did you learn from the pain? How do you think the pain changed you?

CHANGE-O-METER   stayed the same → ① ② ③ ④ ⑤ ← totally different

YOU SUCK

What's the meanest thing you did to someone when you were growing up?

Why did you do it? Who did you do it to? What were the consequences?
Did you ever apologize? Did they ever forgive you? Did it benefit you? Would you do it again?

EXTRA CREDIT

If you never apologized to this person, why not?

If you think it will make them feel better, track them down and offer them a sincere apology. (Don't apologize if you're only doing it to make yourself feel better).

YOU SUCK

What's the meanest thing you have done to someone as an adult?

Why did you do it? Who did you do it to? What were the consequences?
Did you ever apologize? Did they ever forgive you? Did it benefit you? Would you do it again?

PEOPLE ARE AWESOME

What was the kindest, most selfless thing a friend or classmate did for you when you were growing up?

What was your relationship with this person and why do you think they did it? How did it make you feel?
How did it change your relationship with them? Did you ever properly thank them?
What did you learn from this person's act of kindness? Did you change anything about you?

EXTRA CREDIT

If you never properly thanked this person, why not do so now?

Track them down and send them a nice thank-you note.

PEOPLE ARE AWESOME

What is the kindest, most selfless thing a friend, acquaintance, or co-worker has done for you in the past few years?

What is your relationship with this person? How did they help you? How did it make you feel? How did it change your relationship? Did you ever properly thank them? What did you learn from their act of kindness?

If you never properly thanked this person, what's stopping you?

Track them down and send them a nice thank-you note.

YOU ARE AWESOME

What is the kindest, most selfless thing you ever did for a friend or classmate growing up?

What was your relationship with this person? Why did you perform this selfless act? What happened as a result? How do you think it made them feel? How did they respond—did they ever thank you? Did it change your relationship? Did you continue doing selfless acts, or was it not worth it?

YOU ARE AWESOME

What is the kindest, most selfless thing you've done for a friend, acquaintance, or coworker in the past few years?

What is your relationship with this person? Why did you do this gesture? How did they respond?
Did they ever thank you? How did it impact your relationship?
Have you continued to make gestures like this?

CLUBS

List all the groups, clubs, teams, or extracurricular activities you were part of growing up such as chess club, debate, or glee.

Which ones did you like best? What did these groups or clubs mean to you?
Which ones did you hate? Why did you feel that way about them?

List all the clubs you wanted to join
but didn't. What stopped you?

CLUBS

List all the groups, clubs, teams, or regular social groups you're part of now such as game night, book club, or community choir.

How do you like them? Which ones do you like best? What do you get out of them?

EXTRA CREDIT

List all the clubs you've thought about joining as an adult. What's stopping you?

CHANGE-O-METER   stayed the same → (1) (2) (3) (4) (5) ← totally different

MY BIRTHDAY PARTY

Birthday parties are totally (sometimes) awesome! Describe
two of your most memorable birthday parties growing up. And
if you can't remember any, it's possible you partied too hard.

Age: _____

What did you do: _____

_____

How many people came: _____

What part of the party did you care most about (cake,

presents, friends, a crush): _____

What was most memorable about the party: _____

_____

Rate the party from 1 to 5 by
drawing candles on this cake icon:

Age: _____

What did you do: _____

_____

How many people came: _____

What part of the party did you care most about (cake,

presents, friends, a crush): _____

What was most memorable about the party: _____

_____

Rate the party from 1 to 5 by
drawing candles on this cake icon:

MY BIRTHDAY PARTY

Whether or not you want to admit it, you still have a birthday every single year. Rate some of the most recent ones.

This year I turned:

What did you do:

| Rate the party from 1 to 5 by drawing candles on this cake icon: |

How many people came:

What part of the celebration did you care most about

(cake, presents, friends, a crush):

What was most memorable about the party:

Age:

What did you do:

| Rate the party from 1 to 5 by drawing candles on this cake icon: |

How many people came:

What part of the celebration did you care most about

(cake, presents, friends, a crush):

What was most memorable about the party:

CHANGE-O-METER   stayed the same → ① ② ③ ④ ⑤ ← totally different

CENTER OF ATTENTION

Introvert vs. Extrovert

At school dances, did you shake your thang or sit on the sidelines?

When speaking in public (class, church, etc.), did you panic or persevere?

How many people were in the audience at your biggest speech?

What were your strategies or bodily reactions when faced with public speaking?

At parties and social gatherings, did you stick by yourself, hang with friends in a corner, talk to everyone, or avoid going altogether?

Did you crave or hate getting showered with attention?

Did you ever perform (plays, concerts, etc.) in public?

How many people were in the audience at your biggest public performance?

Circle all the types of performances you did growing up, or add your own:

Plays   Musicals   School Band   Garage Band   Circus   Dance   Improve   Poetry Reading

Other:

CENTER OF ATTENTION

Introvert vs. Extrovert

At weddings, parties, and nightclubs, do you shake your thang or stay seated?

When speaking in public (work, church, etc.), do you panic or persevere?

How many people were in the audience at your biggest speech?

What are your strategies or bodily reactions when faced with public speaking?

At parties and social gatherings, do you stick by yourself, hang with friends in a corner, chat everyone up, or stay home and watch Netflix?

Do you crave or hate being showered with attention?

Do you ever perform (plays, concerts, etc.) in public?

How many people were in the audience at your biggest public performance as an adult?

Circle all the types of performances you do these days, or add your own: Community Theatre Community Musicals   Work Band   Garage Band   Circus   Blue Man Group   Open Mic   Karaoke   American Ninja Warrior   Other:

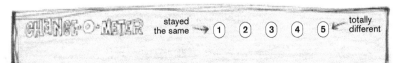 stayed the same → ① ② ③ ④ ⑤ ← totally different

FIGHT CLUB

What was your worst fight growing up, and what was it about?

Who was it with? What was it about? What was it REALLY about? What was the worst moment? How did it resolve? How did it impact your relationship? How did it impact you?

FIGHT CLUB

What was your worst fight in the past year, and what was it about?

Who was it with? What was it about? What was it REALLY about? What was the worst moment? How did it resolve? How did it impact your relationship? How did it impact you?

KEEPIN' IT PHONY

In high school, what did you change about yourself in order to fit in, be accepted, or be popular?

Did you hide parts of your identity or act "fake" in any way? Did you dress differently, talk differently? Which parts of your personality did you exaggerate or minimize? Did you lie or embellish anything about yourself? Was this "social persona" effective or not? Did you like being that other version of yourself?

KEEPIN' IT PHONY

These days, what do you change about yourself in order to fit in, be accepted, or be popular?

Do you hide parts of your identity or act "fake" in any way? Do you dress differently, talk differently? Which parts of your personality do you exaggerate or minimize? Do you lie or embellish anything about yourself? Is this "social persona" effective or not? Do you like being that other version of yourself?

 stayed the same → ① ② ③ ④ ⑤ ← totally different

DESERT ISLAND COMPANIONS

If your teenage self had been stranded on a desert island, which people—dead, living, family, friends, lovers, enemies, celebrities, fictitious characters, etc.—would you have wanted there with you most?

	Person	Relation	Reason
1			
2			
3			
4			
5			

DESERT ISLAND COMPANIONS

If you got stranded on a desert island today, which people—
dead, living, family, friends, lovers, enemies, celebrities, fictitious
characters, etc.—would you want there with you most?

	Person	Relation	Reason
1			
2			
3			
4			
5			

CHAPTER SUMMARY

Congratulations! You finished this chapter.

Now comes the fun part—figure out how much you've changed.
Are you proof that good things always stay the same, like Betty White?
Or are you proof of the power of transformation, like David Bowie?

CALCULATE YOUR SCORE!

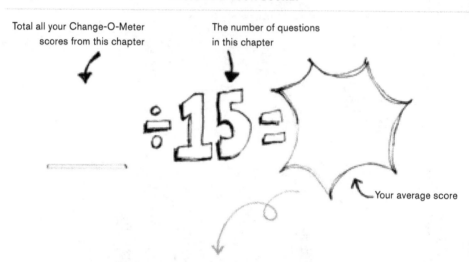

Total all your Change-O-Meter scores from this chapter

The number of questions in this chapter

Your average score

ARE YOU A BETTY OR A BOWIE?
CIRCLE WHERE YOU FALL ON THE SPECTRUM BELOW

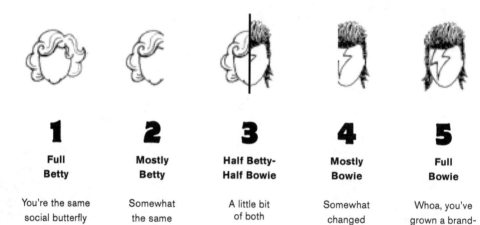

1	**2**	**3**	**4**	**5**
Full Betty	Mostly Betty	Half Betty-Half Bowie	Mostly Bowie	Full Bowie
You're the same social butterfly (or moth) you were as a kid	Somewhat the same	A little bit of both	Somewhat changed	Whoa, you've grown a brand-new pair of butterfly wings!

CHAPTER SUMMARY

What parts of your social life or social persona have changed the least? Did that surprise you?

What parts of your social life or social persona have changed the most? Did that surprise you?

What questions were the hardest to answer in this chapter and why?

Was it harder to answer questions about your childhood or adulthood for this chapter?

What judgments do you have, if any, on the ways you have (and have not) changed?

Do any of these results inspire you to want to change some aspect of your life? If so, what?

INDEX CHAPTER FOUR
POP LIFE?

B

C-60

EVOLUTION OF STYLE

Adolescence is a time for stylistic exploration. Teenagers are "goths" one day and "jocks" the next. Then the following week, they are "emo vintage punk skater-bro hippies." Describe the style that you most closely aligned with in:

7th Grade: _____

Why this style? _____

8th Grade: _____

Why this style? _____

9th Grade: _____

Why this style? _____

10th Grade: _____

Why this style? _____

11 Grade: _____

Why this style? _____

12th Grade: _____

Why this style? _____

EVOLUTION OF STYLE

Believe it or not, adults also go through stylistic changes. You're "yuppy" one day and "cat lady" the next. Describe the most distinct styles you've tried out as an adult.

Style 1: _____

Why this style? _____

_____

Style 2: _____

Why this style? _____

EXTRA CREDIT

Me Now

Draw a picture of your fully accessorized self from your favorite recent style era. Include details such as hairstyle, outfit, accessories—piercings, makeup, slap bracelets, chokers, etc.

Style 3: _____

Why this style? _____

_____

_____

_____

_____

_____

_____

CHANGE-O-METER   stayed the same → ① ② ③ ④ ⑤ ← totally different

SLANG, YO

Alaskans have 100 words for snow. When you were a teen, what other words or phrases did you use for:

Something good: _____

Something bad: _____

Somebody cool: _____

Somebody uncool: _____

Somebody hot: _____

Somebody not hot: _____

A friend: _____

Parties/Events: _____

Currency: _____

Alcohol: _____

Marijuana: _____

Other drugs: _____

Intoxicated: _____

(To) relax: _____

(To) desire: _____

Boys/Men: _____

Girls/Women: _____

A sexual/romantic mate: _____

Penis: _____

Vagina: _____

Breasts: _____

Butt: _____

Kissing/Non-penetrative sex: _____

Fornication: _____

SLANG, YO

Adults have 100 words for aging (growing old, life). What other words or phrases do you currently use for:

Something good:

Something bad:

Somebody cool:

Somebody uncool:

Somebody hot:

Somebody not hot:

A friend:

Parties/Events:

Currency:

Alcohol:

Marijuana:

Other drugs:

Intoxicated:

(To) relax:

(To) desire:

Boys/Men:

Girls/Women:

A sexual/romantic mate:

Penis:

Vagina:

Breasts:

Butt:

Kissing/Non-penetrative sex:

Fornication:

CHANGE-O-METER   stayed the same → (1) (2) (3) (4) (5) ← totally different

ARTS AND CRAFTS

What were your artistic outlets as a kid?

Did you consider yourself to be creative? Did you paint, write stories, shoot videos,
make comic strips, play guitar, code, woodwork, perform? Were you trained or self-taught?
Could you improvise or did you need instructions/notes?

What were your biggest creative
accomplishment(s) growing up?

Example: Slaying lead guitar at a punk show,
getting in a gallery, getting published in the local
paper, being in a play, making home movies,
creating collages, decorating your room, etc.

ARTS AND CRAFTS

What are your artistic outlets today?

Do you consider yourself to be creative now? Do you paint, write stories, shoot videos, make comic strips, play guitar, code, woodwork, perform? Are you trained or self-taught? Can you improvise or do you need instructions/notes?

EXTRA CREDIT

What were your biggest creative accomplishment(s) or products as an adult?

Example: Getting a photograph in a gallery, playing a song at a campfire, performing in community theater, actually completing this journal, creating excellent feng shui in your home, etc.

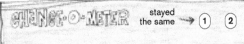

MUSIC TO MY EARS

As a teen, what were your:

Top 10 Albums:

1: _____   6: _____
2: _____   7: _____
3: _____   8: _____
4: _____   9: _____
5: _____   10: _____

Top 10 Bands or Musicians:

1: _____   6: _____
2: _____   7: _____
3: _____   8: _____
4: _____   9: _____
5: _____   10: _____

Top 10 Songs:

1: _____   6: _____
2: _____   7: _____
3: _____   8: _____
4: _____   9: _____
5: _____   10: _____

MUSIC TO MY EARS

As an adult, what are your:

Top 10 Albums:

1: _____   6: _____
2: _____   7: _____
3: _____   8: _____
4: _____   9: _____
5: _____   10: _____

Top 10 Bands or Musicians:

1: _____   6: _____
2: _____   7: _____
3: _____   8: _____
4: _____   9: _____
5: _____   10: _____

Top 10 Songs:

1: _____   6: _____
2: _____   7: _____
3: _____   8: _____
4: _____   9: _____
5: _____   10: _____

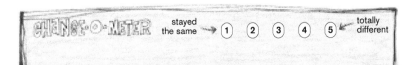

CHANGE-O-METER   stayed the same → ① ② ③ ④ ⑤ ← totally different

THE SCREENING ROOM

What were your favorite movies growing up and what did you love about them?

Favorite Movie #1:

My favorite parts were:

Favorite Movie #2:

My favorite parts were:

Favorite Movie #3:

My favorite parts were:

What were your favorite TV shows growing up and what did you love about them?

Favorite TV Show #1:

My favorite parts were:

Favorite TV Show #2:

My favorite parts were:

Favorite TV Show #3:

My favorite parts were:

EXTRA CREDIT

Check any keywords that describe your interest:

- ☐ I'm Attracted to the Star
- ☐ Stuff Blows Up
- ☐ Someone Cries
- ☐ Someone Dies
- ☐ Fantasy
- ☐ Animal Cast Member
- ☐ Horror
- ☐ Romance
- ☐ Talking Animal or Object
- ☐ Sex Scene
- ☐ Violence
- ☐ Fart Jokes
- ☐ Dick Jokes
- ☐ No Jokes

- ☐ Period Piece
- ☐ Oscar Bid
- ☐ Outer Space
- ☐ Western
- ☐ Crime
- ☐ Sports
- ☐ Big Self-Righteous Speech at the End
- ☐ Courtroom Scene
- ☐ Animated
- ☐ Future
- ☐ Foreign
- ☐ Gritty
- ☐ Family
- ☐ Masturbation Fodder

THE SCREENING ROOM

What are your favorite movies of all time and what do you love about them?

Favorite Movie #1: _____

My favorite parts are: _____

_____

Favorite Movie #2: _____

My favorite parts are: _____

_____

Favorite Movie #3: _____

My favorite parts are: _____

_____

What are your favorite TV shows of all time and what do you love about them?

Favorite TV Show #1: _____

My favorite parts are: _____

_____

Favorite TV Show #2: _____

My favorite parts are: _____

_____

Favorite TV Show #3: _____

My favorite parts are: _____

_____

EXTRA CREDIT

Check any keywords that describe your interest:

- ☐ I'm Attracted to the Star
- ☐ Stuff Blows Up
- ☐ Someone Cries
- ☐ Someone Dies
- ☐ Fantasy
- ☐ Animal Cast Member
- ☐ Horror
- ☐ Romance
- ☐ Talking Animal or Object
- ☐ Sex Scene
- ☐ Violence
- ☐ Fart Jokes
- ☐ Dick Jokes
- ☐ No Jokes

- ☐ Period Piece
- ☐ Oscar Bid
- ☐ Outer Space
- ☐ Western
- ☐ Crime
- ☐ Sports
- ☐ Big Self-Righteous Speech at the End
- ☐ Courtroom Scene
- ☐ Animated
- ☐ Future
- ☐ Foreign
- ☐ Gritty
- ☐ Family
- ☐ Masturbation Fodder

CHANGE-O-METER stayed the same → ① ② ③ ④ ⑤ ← totally different

BOOKWORM

Growing up, what were your favorite books, and what did you love about them? (And yes, comic books count.)

Favorite Book #1: _____

I loved it because: _____

_____

Favorite Book #2: _____

I loved it because: _____

_____

Favorite Book #3: _____

I loved it because: _____

_____

Favorite Book #4: _____

I loved it because: _____

_____

Favorite Book #5: _____

I loved it because: _____

_____

_____

_____

BONUS

What was your favorite magazine or periodical growing up?

BOOKWORM

What are your five favorite books of all time, and what do you love about them? (And yes, manga counts.)

Favorite Book #1:

I love it because:

Favorite Book #2:

I love it because:

Favorite Book #3:

I love it because:

Favorite Book #4:

I love it because:

Favorite Book #5:

I love it because:

BONUS

What is your favorite magazine or periodical these days?

ROCK OUT

My Very First Concert

Headliner:

Opener(s):

Venue and location:

Date/Year:

My Age:

I went with:

I wore:

I drank:

I did (substances):

I remember them playing (list all songs you remember them playing):

My favorite part of the show was:

My least favorite part of the show was:

I got home at:

I was asleep by:

I will always remember:

ROCK OUT

My Most Recent Concert

Headliner:

Opener(s):

Venue and location:

Date/Year:

My Age:

I went with:

I wore:

I drank:

I did (substances):

I remember them playing (list all songs you remember them playing):

My favorite part of the show was:

My least favorite part of the show was:

I got home at:

I was asleep by:

I will always remember:

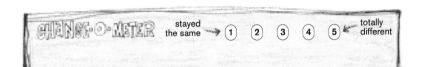

CHANGE-O-METER   stayed the same → (1) (2) (3) (4) (5) ← totally different

CELEBRITY OBSESSIONS

Name five celebrities you admired, idolized, or wanted to totally make out with as a teen.

Who:

Reason:

Who:

Reason:

Who:

Reason:

Who:

Reason:

Who:

Reason:

Now circle your favorite. If you could have spent one evening with that person, what would you have done, and what questions would you have asked them?

CELEBRITY OBSESSIONS

Name five celebrities you currently admire, idolize, or want to "do sex to."

Who:

Reason:

Who:

Reason:

Who:

Reason:

Who:

Reason:

Who:

Reason:

Now circle your favorite. If you could spend one evening with that person, what would you do, and what questions would you ask them?

CHANGE-O-METER stayed the same → ① ② ③ ④ ⑤ ← totally different

Congratulations! You finished this chapter.

Now comes the fun part—figure out how much you've changed.
Are you proof that good things always stay the same, like Betty White?
Or are you proof of the power of transformation, like David Bowie?

CALCULATE YOUR SCORE!

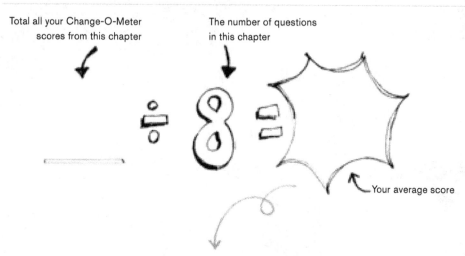

Total all your Change-O-Meter scores from this chapter

The number of questions in this chapter

Your average score

ARE YOU A BETTY OR A BOWIE?
CIRCLE WHERE YOU FALL ON THE SPECTRUM BELOW

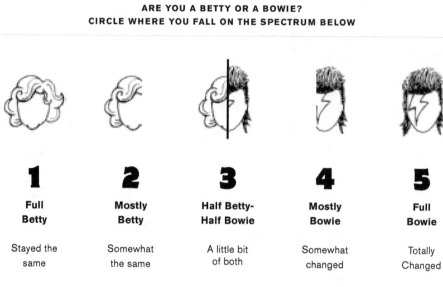

1	**2**	**3**	**4**	**5**
Full Betty	Mostly Betty	Half Betty-Half Bowie	Mostly Bowie	Full Bowie
Stayed the same	Somewhat the same	A little bit of both	Somewhat changed	Totally Changed

CHAPTER SUMMARY

What parts of your pop life have changed the least? Did that surprise you?

What parts of your pop life have changed the most? Did that surprise you?

What questions were the hardest to answer in this chapter and why?

Was it harder to answer about your childhood or adulthood for this chapter?

What judgments do you have, if any, on the ways you have (and have not) changed?

Do any of these results inspire you to want to change some aspect of your life? If so, what?

CHAPTER FIVE

My Mortified Faith

OH MY GOD

What were your beliefs about God growing up?

Did God exist? Did you believe in multiple Gods? Did God have rules? Did God watch you? Did God communicate with you? How did your belief give you comfort, if at all?

OH MY GOD

What are your current beliefs about God?

Does God exist? Do you believe in multiple Gods? Does God have rules? Does God watch you?
Does God communicate with you? How does your belief give you comfort, if at all?

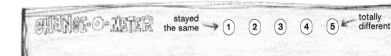

HAPPILY EVER AFTERLIFE

Did you believe in the afterlife growing up?

What did it look like? Did your belief comfort you, scare you, or creep you out, and why?
What was the criteria, if any, for getting into the afterlife? Did you believe in reincarnation?

HAPPILY EVER AFTERLIFE

What are your current beliefs about the afterlife?

What does it look like? Do your beliefs comfort you, scare you, or creep you out, and why?
What is the criteria, if any, for getting into the afterlife? Do you believe in reincarnation?

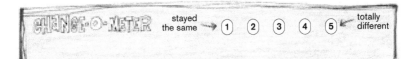

WORSHIP ME

How often did you worship or engage in a spiritual activity growing up—be it a prayer, ceremony, or ritual?

What was it? Why did you do it or not do it? How often did you engage in this activity?

WORSHIP ME

How often do you worship or engage in a spiritual activity as an adult—be it a prayer, ceremony or ritual?

What is it? Why do you do it or not do it? How often do you engage in this activity?

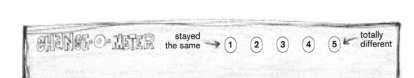

DEAD HEAD

Growing up, how did you deal with death?

What was your experience with death? Were you ever impacted by it?
Did you express emotion about it? Were you nonchalant about it?

DEAD HEAD

How have you dealt with death as an adult?

What is your experience with death? Do you express emotions about it?
Are you nonchalant about it?

DIY TOMBSTONE

Imagine your teenage self had been tasked with writing
your tombstone. What would they have written?

DIY TOMBSTONE

If you were tasked with writing your tombstone
now, what would you write?

SPIRIT ANIMAL

Draw your teenage spirit animal.

It doesn't have to be real. It can be extinct, mythological, legendary, completely made-up, or a crazy combination of a bunch of different awesome animals.

SPIRIT ANIMAL

Draw your spirit animal.

It doesn't have to be real. It can be extinct, mythological, legendary, completely made-up, or an awesome combination of a bunch of different crazy animals.

YOU ARE MY SHEPHERD

Did you ever turn to a spiritual leader for guidance, growing up? If so, who?

Was it someone you knew in person, through a book, the media, or somewhere else?
Why did you find this person so appealing? What were their core beliefs?
Did you view this person as flawless? Did you ever turn against this person?

YOU ARE MY SHEPHERD

Do you ever turn to a spiritual leader for guidance, today? If so, who?

Is it someone you know in person, through a book, the media, or somewhere else?
Why do you find this person appealing? What are their core
beliefs? Have you ever turned against this person?

NOW AND ZEN

Growing up, what did you do when you wanted to tune out the world and mentally escape?

Did you journal, cuddle with your dog, play on a tire swing, watch clouds, lie on the carpet and draw?
How often did you do this? How long did these escapes take—minutes, hours?
How did this form of escape help you? Do you still do this, today?

NOW AND ZEN

These days, what do you do when you want to tune out the world and escape into something, almost achieving a zen state of mind?

Do you meditate, journal, drive, hike, hit the gym? How often do you do this?
How long do these escapes take—minutes, hours? How does this form of escape help you?

Congratulations! You finished this chapter.

Now comes the fun part—figure out how much you've changed.
Are you proof that good things always stay the same, like Betty White?
Or are you proof of the power of transformation, like David Bowie?

CALCULATE YOUR SCORE!

Total all your Change-O-Meter scores from this chapter

The number of questions in this chapter

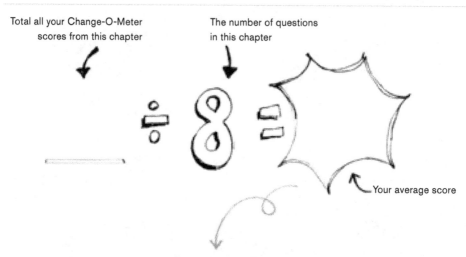

Your average score

ARE YOU A BETTY OR A BOWIE?
CIRCLE WHERE YOU FALL ON THE SPECTRUM BELOW

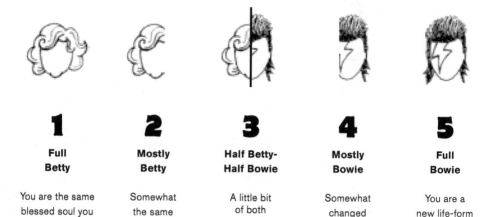

1	2	3	4	5
Full Betty	**Mostly Betty**	**Half Betty-Half Bowie**	**Mostly Bowie**	**Full Bowie**
You are the same blessed soul you were as a child	Somewhat the same	A little bit of both	Somewhat changed	You are a new life-form descended from the heavens on a trail of rainbows

CHAPTER SUMMARY

What parts of your faith have changed the least? Did that surprise you?

What parts of your faith have changed the most? Did that surprise you?

What questions were the hardest to answer in this chapter and why?

Was it harder to answer about your childhood or adulthood for this chapter?

What judgments do you have, if any, on the ways you have (and have not) changed?

Do any of these results inspire you to want to change some aspect of your life? If so, what?

Ch 06

Worker

Bee

A'S AND F'S

What was the school subject you most excelled in as a kid?

Why did you excel in that? Did you enjoy it? Why or why not?
What did you learn in that subject that you still use or think about, today?

_____

_____

_____

_____

_____

_____

What was the school subject you least excelled in as a kid, and why?

_____

_____

_____

_____

_____

_____

_____

_____

_____

_____

A'S AND F'S

If you were to receive an "A" grade for something you know a LOT about as an adult, what would that be?

Why do you excel in that? Do you enjoy it? Why or why not? How long have you been good at this?

If you were to receive an "F" grade for something you do as an adult, what would that be? Why?

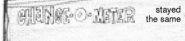

HIGHLIGHTS

What was your favorite part of your school day?

Why did you love it? What was the highlight of doing that? How long did it last?
Were you with anyone or alone—and if the former, who? What was your least favorite part of the day?

Who were your three favorite teachers growing up, and why were they your favorites?

Teacher name and subject:

I loved this teacher because:

Teacher name and subject:

I loved this teacher because:

Teacher name and subject:

I loved this teacher because:

HIGHLIGHTS

What is your favorite part of your work day?

Why do you love it? What is the highlight of doing that? How long does it last?
Are you with anyone or alone—and if the former, who? What is your least favorite part of the day?

Who are your 3 favorite coworkers or bosses, and why?

Coworker name and role:

I love this coworker because:

Coworker name and role:

I love this coworker because:

Coworker name and role:

I love this coworker because:

COLLABORATION

Growing up, did you prefer to do work in groups or solo?

Why did you prefer this? Can you recall a life event that serves as an example of why you preferred this? Describe a moment where this preference helped you shine.

COLLABORATION

As an adult, would you rather do work with a group or solo?

Why do you prefer this? Can you recall a life event that serves as an example of why you prefer this? Describe a moment where this preference has helped you shine. How is your preference as a kid similar to your preference now? Likewise, how do they differ?

stayed the same → ① ② ③ ④ ⑤ ← totally different

FOLLOW THE LEADER

In school, did you consider yourself a leader, a follower, or something in between?

Why did you fall into this role? Were you frequently in this role in all areas of your life, or did you fluctuate depending on the circumstances? Did you prefer to occupy this role, or did you want to switch? What judgments did you have of people who occupied the other role?

FOLLOW THE LEADER

In the workplace, do you consider yourself a leader, a follower, or something else?

Why do you fall into this role, today? Do you always fall into this role? Do you prefer to occupy this role, or would you rather switch? Do you believe it is best for people to follow their own path? What judgments do you have of people who occupy the other role? How is your role as a kid similar to your role now? Likewise, how do they differ?

EMBARRASSMENT 101

What was your most mortifying memory of school?

Why was it embarrassing? Where did it happen? How long did it haunt
you? Did people laugh at you? Does it still made you shudder?

　　　　　　MY MORTIFIED LIFE

EMBARRASSMENT 101

What is the most mortifying moment you've had in the workplace?

Why was it embarrassing? Where did it happen? Does it haunt you? Did people laugh at you? Does it still make you shudder? Which felt worse in the moment: your childhood embarrassment or your adult one?

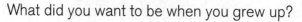

CONGRATULATIONS, YOU'RE HIRED!

What did you want to be when you grew up?

Why was this your dream career? Which skills did this profession require, and which of those skills did you actually have? In what ways did you pursue this career? Do you continue to pursue it? If not, when and why did it stop being a goal?

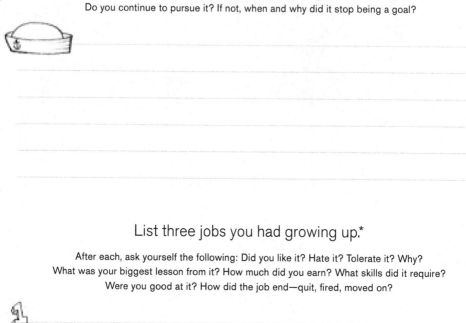

List three jobs you had growing up.*

After each, ask yourself the following: Did you like it? Hate it? Tolerate it? Why? What was your biggest lesson from it? How much did you earn? What skills did it require? Were you good at it? How did the job end—quit, fired, moved on?

 1

 2

 3

* If you had less than 3 jobs, consider yourself a payroll unicorn.

CONGRATULATIONS, YOU'RE HIRED!

What is your current occupation?

How is it satisfying? How is it unsatisfying? Which skills of yours does it require?
How is it similar to your childhood dream job, and how does it differ?

List two other jobs you've had as an adult.*

After each, ask yourself the following: Did you like it? Hate it? Tolerate it?
Why? What was your biggest lesson from it? How much did you earn? What skills did
it require? Were you good at it? How did the job end—quit, fired, moved on?

SUPERHERO VS. SLOTH

Growing up, were you generally a hard worker or were you lazy?

Why do you believe you were this way? Were you this way in all areas, or did it
fluctuate depending on the task? Did you like this aspect of yourself?

SUPERHERO VS. SLOTH

As a grown-up, are you generally a hard worker or are you lazy?

And if you're lazy, make room for us on the couch! What makes you this way? Do you like this aspect of yourself? Are you this way in all areas, or does it fluctuate depending on the task? How is your degree of motivation today similar to your motivation levels growing up, and how does it differ?

 stayed the same → (1) (2) (3) (4) (5) ← totally different

CHAPTER SUMMARY

Congratulations! You finished this chapter.

Now comes the fun part— figure out how much you've changed. Are you proof that good things always stay the same, like Betty White? Or are you proof of the power of transformation, like David Bowie?

CALCULATE YOUR SCORE!

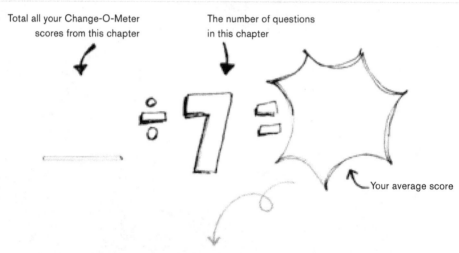

Total all your Change-O-Meter scores from this chapter

The number of questions in this chapter

Your average score

ARE YOU A BETTY OR A BOWIE?
CIRCLE WHERE YOU FALL ON THE SPECTRUM BELOW

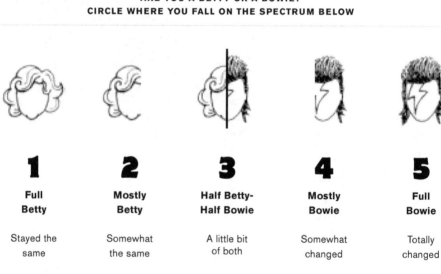

1	**2**	**3**	**4**	**5**
Full Betty	**Mostly Betty**	**Half Betty- Half Bowie**	**Mostly Bowie**	**Full Bowie**
Stayed the same	Somewhat the same	A little bit of both	Somewhat changed	Totally changed

CHAPTER SUMMARY

What parts of your work life have changed the least? Did that surprise you?

What parts of your work life have changed the most? Did that surprise you?

What questions were the hardest to answer in this chapter and why?

Was it harder to answer about your childhood or adulthood for this chapter?

What judgments do you have, if any, on the ways you have (and have not) changed?

Do any of these results inspire you to want to change some aspect of your life? If so, what?

CHAPTER 7

MY SO-called LIFESTYLE

WEEKDAYS VS. WEEKENDS

Write your typical schedule from when you were young—be it as a kid or teenager.

Time	Weekday	Weekend
6 am - 8 am		
8 am - 10 am		
10 am - 1 pm		
1 pm - 4 pm		
4 pm - 7 pm		
7 pm - 10 pm		
10 pm - 12 am		
12 am - 2 am		
2 am - 6 am		

What was your favorite part & why?

WEEKDAYS VS. WEEKENDS

Write your typical schedule today.

Time	Weekday	Weekend
6 am - 8 am		
8 am - 10 am		
10 am - 1 pm		
1 pm - 4 pm		
4 pm - 7 pm		
7 pm - 10 pm		
10 pm - 12 am		
12 am - 2 am		
2 am - 6 am		

What is your favorite part & why?

THE END OF THE DAY

When you were growing up, what did you typically do after school?

Did you usually hang out with other kids or go straight home? Did you do homework or play outside? Did you have a snack? A smoke? Play sports? Play Sega? What did you love about these activities?

MY MORTIFIED LIFE

THE END OF THE DAY

Nowadays, what do you typically do after work?

Do you usually hang out with coworkers or friends, or do you go straight home?
Do you go on dates? Do you take your work home? How do you unwind—eat,
smoke, meditate, Pilates? What did you love about these activities?

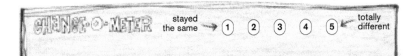

EXERCISE

My primary form(s) of exercise growing up involved...

Why did you exercise? How frequently did you exercise? Did you enjoy it?
What did you do to avoid it if you didn't like it?

EXERCISE

My primary form(s) of exercise today involve...

Why do you exercise? How frequently do you exercise?
Do you enjoy it? What do you do to avoid it if you don't like it?

TASTE BUDS

My Daily Diet

My favorite food was: _____

My favorite dessert was: _____

My favorite fruit was: _____

My favorite vegetable was: _____

My favorite breakfast food was: _____

My favorite lunch food was: _____

My favorite dinner was: _____

The grossest food I loved was: _____

I hated eating: _____

I refused to eat: _____

My parents forced me to eat: _____

My parents didn't let me eat: _____

On my birthday, I asked for: _____ as the main course.

On my birthday, I asked for: _____ cake.

On Halloween, my favorite candy was: _____

My favorite holiday meal was: _____

It consisted of: _____

If I had to choose one thing to eat for every meal, for the rest of my life, it would obviously have

been:

TASTE BUDS

My Daily Diet

My favorite food is: _____

My favorite dessert is: _____

My favorite fruit is: _____

My favorite vegetable is: _____

My favorite breakfast food is: _____

My favorite lunch food is: _____

My favorite dinner is: _____

The grossest food I love is: _____

I hate eating: _____

I refuse to eat: _____

I force myself to eat: _____

I force myself not to eat: _____

On my birthday, I want: _____ as the main course.

On my birthday, I want: _____ cake.

My favorite treat is: _____

My favorite holiday meal is: _____

It consists of: _____

If I had to choose one thing to eat for every meal, for the rest of my life, it would obviously be:

_____

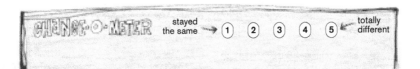

CHANGE-O-METER   stayed the same → ① ② ③ ④ ⑤ ← totally different   155

HAPPY DAY

What was the best moment of your entire childhood or adolescence, and what made it so memorable?

What happened? Who were you with? Why was it so awesome?
What do you remember most about that day?

156   MY MORTIFIED LIFE

HAPPY DAY

What is the best moment of your entire adulthood, and what makes it so memorable?

What happened? Who were you with? Why was it so awesome?
What do you remember most about that day?

 stayed the same → (1) (2) (3) (4) (5) ← totally different

157

WORST DAY

What was the worst day of your entire childhood or adolescence, and what made it so bad?

Who were you with? Are you grateful for it? What did it teach you?

WORST DAY

What was the worst day of your adult life, and what made it so bad?

Who were you with? Are you grateful for it? What did it teach you?

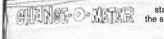 stayed the same ➔ (1) (2) (3) (4) (5) ↞ totally different

FOREVER YOUNG (OR PERMANENTLY OLD)

If your childhood or teenage self had to choose one age to be forever, what age would you have chosen and why?

Was it an age from childhood, or an age you couldn't wait to be? If it was a childhood age, what was so great about it? If it was an adult age, why did you expect that age to be so awesome?

FOREVER YOUNG (OR PERMANENTLY OLD)

If you had to choose one age to be forever, what age would you choose and why?

Is it an age you've already lived, or an age you can't wait to be? If it's an age from your past, what was so great about that age? If it's a future age, what do you think that age will be like?

HEROES

Who did you look up to the most, growing up?

What did you admire about them? Did you know them personally?
How have they impacted your life?

HEROES

Who do you look up to the most, today?

What do you admire about them? When did they become your hero?
Do you know them personally? How have they impacted your life?

DON'T TURN OFF THE LIGHT!

What was your biggest fear growing up and why?

Was it real, rational, distorted, imagined? What was the origin?

DON'T TURN OFF THE LIGHT!

What is your biggest fear as an adult and why?

Is it real, rational, distorted, imagined? What is the origin?

LATEST CRAZE

List all the trends, novelties, or crazes you got swept up in growing up.

Example: Lava lamps, pet rocks, mood rings, bean bag chairs, dance crazes, catch phrases, wearing friendship bracelets, dressing emo, participating in "Hands Across America." Were you an early adopter, part of the herd, or a latecomer? Why did you get caught up in this trend?

EXTRA CREDIT

What was your biggest collection growing up?

(baseball cards, stamps, Beanie Babies, etc.)

LATEST CRAZE

List all the trends, novelties, or crazes you've gotten swept up in as an adult.

Example: Wearing Google Glasses, doing the Ice Bucket Challenge, planking, participating in a flash mob, South Beach diet. Were you an early adopter, part of the herd, or a latecomer? Why did you get caught up in it?

What is your biggest collection these days?

(vintage cars, vintage clothing, recipes, etc.)

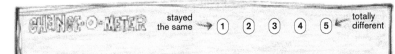

BIRTHDAY GIFT

What was the #1 birthday gift you wanted as a little kid but never got? How about as a teenager?

Why did you want it? Why did you never get it as a kid? Did you
ever get it later? What lengths did you go to get it?

MY MORTIFIED LIFE

BIRTHDAY GIFT

What is the #1 thing you want for your birthday this year that you've never had?

Why do you want it? Why have you never received it? What lengths have you gone to get it?

stayed the same → ① ② ③ ④ ⑤ ← totally different

RESCUE MISSION

Hurry! Your childhood home is on fire and you can only
rescue five items. What items do you grab and why?*

1

2

3

4

5

What if you only had time to grab one item?

* Don't worry, everybody's totally safe and your insurance is totally awesome.

RESCUE MISSION

Hurry! Your current home in on fire, and you can only rescue five items. What items do you grab and why?*

1

2

3

4

5

What if you only had time to grab one item?

MY MORTIFIED HOBBIES

List all the hobbies you tried when growing up, such as knitting or keeping a diary.

Which ones did you like best? Worst? Why? Which ones did you actually keep up?

MY MORTIFIED HOBBIES

List all the hobbies you've tried as an adult.

Which ones have you liked best? Worst? Why? Which ones have you actually kept up?

List any creative outlets or hobbies you've been
intending to try out. Go out and try one!

 stayed the same → ① ② ③ ④ ⑤ ← totally different

Congratulations! You finished this chapter.

Now comes the fun part—figure out how much you've changed.
Are you proof that good things always stay the same, like Betty White?
Or are you proof of the power of transformation, like David Bowie?

CALCULATE YOUR SCORE!

Total all your Change-O-Meter scores from this chapter

The number of questions in this chapter

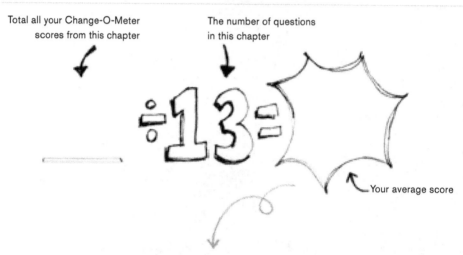

Your average score

ARE YOU A BETTY OR A BOWIE?
CIRCLE WHERE YOU FALL ON THE SPECTRUM BELOW

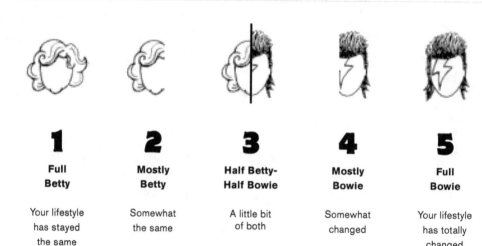

1	**2**	**3**	**4**	**5**
Full Betty	**Mostly Betty**	**Half Betty-Half Bowie**	**Mostly Bowie**	**Full Bowie**
Your lifestyle has stayed the same	Somewhat the same	A little bit of both	Somewhat changed	Your lifestyle has totally changed

MY MORTIFIED LIFE

What parts of your lifestyle have changed the least? Did that surprise you?

What parts of your lifestyle have changed the most? Did that surprise you?

What questions were the hardest to answer in this chapter and why?

Was it harder to answer about your childhood or adulthood for this chapter?

What judgments do you have, if any, on the ways you have (and have not) changed?

Do any of these results inspire you to want to change some aspect of your life? If so, what?

Chapter Eight

If I Ruled the World

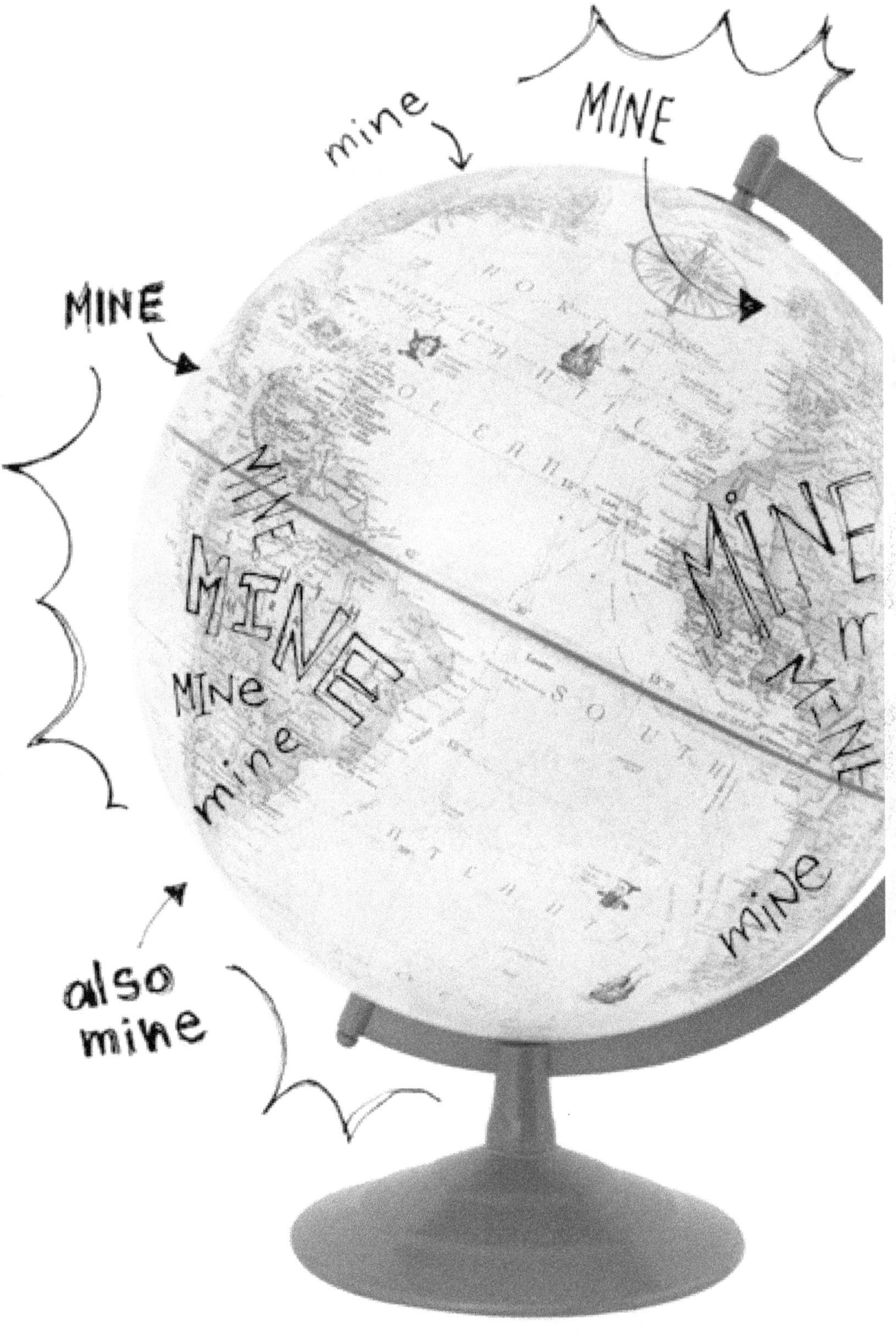
mine
MINE
MINE
MINE
MINE
MINE
Mine
mine
MINE
MINE
mine
also mine

CHANGING THE WORLD

Growing up, if you could have changed one thing about the world, what would you have changed and why?

CHANGING THE WORLD

Nowadays, if you could change one thing about the world, what would you change and why?

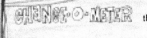

CAUSE

What social movements or issues, such as poverty, the environment, and civil rights, were you most passionate about growing up?

What did you do to fight? If you could go back, would you do anything differently?

CAUSE

Over the last few years, what social movements or issues, such as LGBTQ rights, global warming, or unemployment, are you most passionate about?

What have you done to fight? What issues do you wish you could fight more for?

 stayed the same → (1)(2)(3)(4)(5) totally different

SUPERPOWER

What superpower did you want growing up?

Why was that your fantasy compared to other powers?
What do you think that says about your needs as a kid?

Draw your superhero character:

SUPERPOWER

What superpower would you want as an adult?

Why is this your fantasy compared to other powers? What do you think that says about you?
If your fantasy changed from childhood, why do you think that is?

Draw your superhero character:

T-SHIRT PHILOSOPHY

If your teenage philosophy was condensed into a T-shirt slogan and design, what would it say and look like?

Why was that your slogan? What would it say on the backside of the shirt?
Design the T-shirt, including slogans, using the image below.

FRONT

BACK

T-SHIRT PHILOSOPHY

If your current philosophy was condensed into a slogan and design on a T-shirt, what would it say and look like?

Why is that your slogan? What would it say on the backside of the shirt?
Design the T-shirt, including slogans, using the image below.

FRONT

BACK

CHANGE-O-METER   stayed the same → ① ② ③ ④ ⑤ ← totally different

185

SPENDER

If you got $2,500 for selling the most Girl Scout cookies of anyone in troop #281, what would you have spent it on and why?

How long would it have lasted? How many things would you have bought with this— one big thing, a few medium-priced things, or lots of little things? Would you have spent it on something pragmatic or pure fun?

Same question, but this time you got $1,000,000. What would you have done?

SPENDER

If you got a $2,500 bonus at work for sucking up to the boss, what would you spend it on and why?

How long would it last? How many things would you buy with this—one big thing, a few medium-priced things, or lots of little things? Would you spend it on something pragmatic or pure fun? What is similar about your adult answer and your childhood answer? What is different?

Same question, but this time you get $1,000,000. What do you do?

MAKING HISTORY

If your teenage self could spend a day with any historical figure, who would you choose and why?

Why them? What did you like about them? What would you spend
the day doing? What would you ask them?

MAKING HISTORY

If your current self had the opportunity to spend the day with any historical figure, who would you choose and why?

Why them? What do you like about them? What would you spend the day doing? What would you ask them? What similarities do you notice between your answers from adulthood versus childhood? What differences do you notice?

VOTING VIA TIME TRAVEL

If your teenage self could have voted in the most recent presidential election, who would little you have voted for and why?

What would your teenage self have loved about that candidate? What would your teenage self have hated about the opposing candidate? What would you have thought about any of the scandals?

VOTING VIA TIME TRAVEL

If you could vote today in one presidential election that happened in your teenage years, which election would you choose, who would your adult self vote for, and why?

What do you love about that candidate? What do dislike about the opposing candidate? How do your childhood and adult politics differ? How are they similar?

 stayed the same → (1) (2) (3) (4) (5) ← totally different

Congratulations! You finished this chapter.

Now comes the fun part—figure out how much you've changed.
Are you proof that good things always stay the same, like Betty White?
Or are you proof of the power of transformation, like David Bowie?

CALCULATE YOUR SCORE!

Total all your Change-O-Meter
scores from this chapter

The number of questions
in this chapter

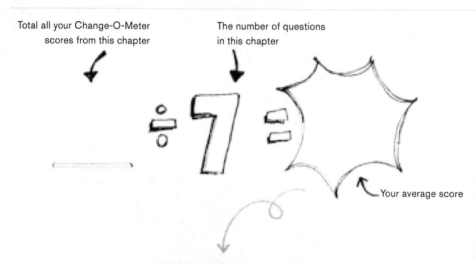

Your average score

ARE YOU A BETTY OR A BOWIE?
CIRCLE WHERE YOU FALL ON THE SPECTRUM BELOW

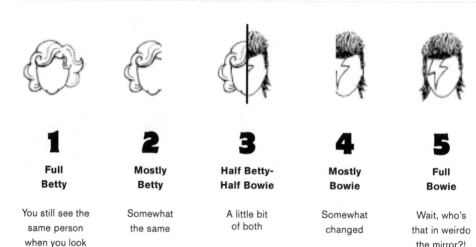

1	**2**	**3**	**4**	**5**
Full Betty	Mostly Betty	Half Betty- Half Bowie	Mostly Bowie	Full Bowie
You still see the same person when you look in the mirror	Somewhat the same	A little bit of both	Somewhat changed	Wait, who's that in weirdo the mirror?!

CHAPTER SUMMARY

What parts of your world views have changed the least? Did that surprise you?

What parts of your world views have changed the most? Did that surprise you?

What questions were the hardest to answer in this chapter and why?

Was it harder to answer about your childhood or adulthood for this chapter?

What judgments do you have, if any, on the ways you have (and have not) changed?

Do any of these results inspire you to want to change some aspect of your life? If so, what?

Chapter Nine

MY FIERY CONFIDENCE

What did you love most about yourself growing up, and why?

Was it a skill or a physical trait? An aspect of your personality? Something about your style? Was this awesome trait super unique or did other people have it? How did it affect your life— did you get praise or special attention? Did you show off or brag, or were you humble?

MY FIERY CONFIDENCE

What do you love most about yourself today, and why?

Is it a skill or a physical trait? An aspect of your personality? Something about your style?
Is this awesome trait super unique or do other people have this trait? How does it affect
your life—do you get praise or special attention? Do you show off, or brag, or are you
humble about it? If your source of pride has changed, why do you think that is?

CHANGE-O-METER   stayed the same ➔ ① ② ③ ④ ⑤ ← totally different

MY BURNING INSECURITIES

What was your #1 biggest insecurity growing up, and why were you so insecure about it?

How did it affect your decisions? Did you ever talk about this insecurity with anybody? Who?
How often? How'd it go/feel? Looking back, do you think a lot of other people had similar insecurities?

MY BURNING INSECURITIES

What is your #1 biggest insecurity these days, and why are you so insecure about it?

How does it affect your decisions? Do you ever talk about this insecurity with anybody? Who? How often? How'd it go/feel? Do you think a lot of other people have similar insecurities?

MY VANITY MIRROR

What part of your body did you love the most, growing up?

Why did you love it so much? How did you show it off? How often did you think about it?
How did it affect your life?

draw it here

What part of your body did you hate the most, growing up?

Why did you dislike it so much? Did you ever hide it? How often
did you think about it? How did it affect your life?

draw it here

MY VANITY MIRROR

What part of your body do you love the most, as an adult?

Why do you love it so much? How do you show it off? How often do you think about it?
How does it affect your life?

 draw it here

What part of your body do you hate the most, as an adult?

Why do you dislike it so much? Do you ever hide it? How often do
you think about it? How does it affect your life?

draw it here

What was your most annoying personality trait?

Did you even notice when you were acting like that? How did people react to it?
How did it impact your life? How did you learn to stop, if you ever did?

MY MORTIFYING PERSONALITY

What's your most annoying personality trait?

Do you even notice when you act like that? How do people react to it? How does it impact your life?

MY SWISS ARMY KNIFE OF AWESOMENESS

Imagine that childhood is a forest called The Treacherous Woods of Childhood and you needed a metaphorical Swiss Army knife to survive. What were the five most useful tools you carried on your knife, and how did you develop them?

Instead of thinking of talents like guitar or dance, try to think of the life skills like street smarts, resiliency, or quick-thinking—you know, things that helped you get through tough times or stay out of trouble.

Skill 1:

How I developed it:

Skill 2:

How I developed it:

Skill 3:

How I developed it:

Skill 4:

How I developed it:

Skill 5:

How I developed it:

MY SWISS ARMY KNIFE OF AWESOMENESS

Now imagine adulthood is a place called The Stormy Mountains of Adulthood and you need a completely different metaphorical Swiss Army knife to survive. What are the five most useful tools you can unfold, and how did you develop them?

Again, avoid listing talents and focus on your unique life skills, the qualities that help you get through the day to day trials and tribulations of grown-up life. For example, maybe you have the ability to cheer people up with humor, or maybe you can charm your way up the social ladder, or maybe you have an active imagination that helps you get through tough times.

Skill 1:

How I developed it:

Skill 2:

How I developed it:

Skill 3:

How I developed it:

Skill 4:

How I developed it:

Skill 5:

How I developed it:

stayed the same → (1) (2) (3) (4) (5) ← totally different

205

WIN SOME, LOSE SOME

What was your biggest accomplishment growing up and what work or skills were required to achieve each?

What was your #1 biggest mistake growing up?

Why did you make it? What did it ruin? Who did it affect and how?
How did it impact your life?. How and when did it resolve, if ever? What did you learn from it?

WIN SOME, LOSE SOME

What is your biggest accomplishment as an adult and what work or skills were required to achieve it?

What is your #1 biggest mistake as an adult?

Why did you make this mistake? How does it affect you?
How have you tried to resolve it? What have you learned from it?

 stayed the same → ① ② ③ ④ ⑤ ← totally different

HEY, SHITHEAD!

Growing up, what were some of the worst things people said about you, and why do you think they said them?

Were you called an asshole, a loser, a bitch, a spaz, a skank, a womanizer, a prude, a stoner, a slacker, or a bully? Did you work hard to overcome this reputation, or were you okay with it? What did you do to earn this reputation, if anything?

Conversely, what were some of the best things people said about you, and why did they say them?

Were they about your personality, your looks, your skills, or something else? Did you like this reputation? Did you think you deserved it?

HEY, SHITHEAD!

What are some of the worst things people say about you today, and why do they say them?

Have you been called a jerk, a hellion, a misogynist, a douche-pickle, a workaholic, a disappointment, an alcoholic, a druggy, or an unreasonably genocidal, narcissistic egomaniac? Did you work hard to overcome this reputation, or are you cool with it? Do you think you deserve it?

Conversely, what are some of the best things people say about you, and why do they say them?

Are they about your personality, your looks, your skills, or something else?
Do you like this reputation? Do you think you deserve it?

 stayed the same →   (3) (4)   totally different

209

CHAPTER SUMMARY

Congratulations! You finished this chapter.

Now comes the fun part—figure out how much you've changed.
Are you proof that good things always stay the same, like Betty White?
Or are you proof of the power of transformation, like David Bowie?

CALCULATE YOUR SCORE!

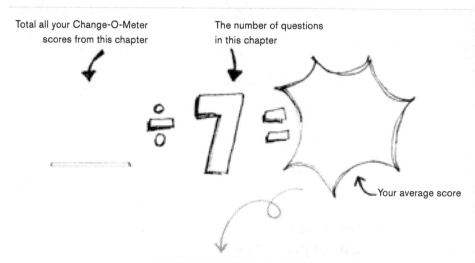

Total all your Change-O-Meter scores from this chapter

The number of questions in this chapter

Your average score

ARE YOU A BETTY OR A BOWIE?
CIRCLE WHERE YOU FALL ON THE SPECTRUM BELOW

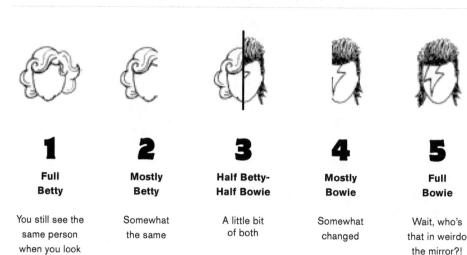

1	2	3	4	5
Full Betty	**Mostly Betty**	**Half Betty- Half Bowie**	**Mostly Bowie**	**Full Bowie**
You still see the same person when you look in the mirror	Somewhat the same	A little bit of both	Somewhat changed	Wait, who's that in weirdo the mirror?!

What parts of your self-esteem have changed the least? Did that surprise you?

What parts of your self-esteem have changed the most? Did that surprise you?

What questions were the hardest to answer in this chapter and why?

Was it harder to answer about your childhood or adulthood for this chapter?

What judgments do you have, if any, on the ways you have (and have not) changed?

Do any of these results inspire you to want to change some aspect of your life? If so, what?

☖

VICE GRIP

What was your #1 vice growing up?

Example: Smoking, lying, drinking, stealing, dirty magazines, junk food, gambling, eating too much hummus, etc. Why did you do it? Did you ever quit? Did it bring you more happiness or misery?

VICE GRIP

What's your #1 vice as an adult?

Why do you do it? Do you think you'll ever quit? Does it bring you more happiness or misery?

 stayed the same →   5 ← totally different

215

DIRTY SECRETS

What was the #1 thing you hid from your family or friends growing up?

Why? How long did you hide it? Were you ever caught and how did you handle it?

What's the worst crime you ever committed as a teen?

Why did you do it? Were you reprimanded?

CRIME SCENE DO NOT ENTER CRIME SCENE

DIRTY SECRETS

What is the #1 thing you hide from your family or friends as an adult?

Why? How long have you hid it? Have you ever been caught and how did you handle that?

What's the worst crime you ever committed as an adult?

Why did you do it? Were you reprimanded?

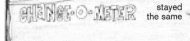

FIGHTING THE LAW

Growing up, what laws or rules such as sneaking out, stealing, cheating on a test, or skipping class did you break in an average week?

Why did you break them? Are you surprised by how many or how few rules
you used to break? Do you suspect your friends behaved similarly?

FIGHTING THE LAW

In the past week, what laws or rules such as not paying parking meters, speeding, stealing a stapler from the office, or taking extended lunch breaks on the job do you think you've broken?

Why did you break them? Are you surprised by how many or how few rules you broke this week? Do you suspect your friends or coworkers behave similarly?

CHANGE-O-METER   stayed the same → ① ② ③ ④ ⑤ ← totally different

🔥

INTOXICATION

When was the first time you got drunk or high as a teenager, if ever?

What was the substance? Why did you do it? Who were you with? How'd you get it?
What was the most memorable moment? Do you wish you had made a different choice?

INTOXICATION

When was the most recent time you got intoxicated, if ever?

What was the substance? Why did you do it? How'd you get it? What was the most memorable moment?
Do you wish you had made a different choice? If you've never been intoxicated, discuss that experience.

 stayed the same → (1) (2) (3) (4) (5) ← totally different

THE (RAPID) FIRES OF HELL

As a teen . . .

I drank about: _____ cups of coffee per month.

I smoked about: _____ cigarettes per month.

I drank about: _____ alcoholic drinks per month.

I smoked weed about: _____ times per month.

When I drank, I usually drank about: _____ drinks in a night.

My favorite drink was: _____ .

My favorite intoxicant was: _____

I tried (list all the illegal drugs you tried at least once): _____

_____

I (somewhat) regularly got high on (list all the drugs you did more than once per year): _____

_____

I got royally fucked up: _____ times per year.

The worst thing I ever stole was: _____

_____

Throughout high school, I smoked roughly: _____ packs of cigarettes in total.

Throughout high school, I drank roughly: _____ beers in total.

Throughout high school, I drank roughly: _____ alcoholic drinks in total.

Throughout high school, I smoked roughly: _____
joints (or blunts, bowls, or bongs) in total.

I did about: _____ pounds of drugs.

In conclusion, I am: _____ going to hell.

THE (RAPID) FIRES OF HELL

These days . . .

I drink about: _____ cups of coffee per month.

I smoke about: _____ cigarettes per month.

I drink about: _____ alcoholic drinks per month.

I smoke weed about: _____ times per month.

When I drink, I usually drink about: _____ drinks in a night.

My favorite drink is: _____ .

My favorite intoxicant is: _____

I occasionally try (list all the illegal drugs you do occasionally): _____

_____

I (somewhat) regularly get high on (list all the drugs you do more than once per year): _____

_____

I get absolutely smashed about: _____ times per year.

The worst thing I've stolen in the past 5 years was: _____

_____

As an adult, I've smoked roughly: _____ packs of cigarettes in total.

As an adult, I've drank roughly: _____ beers in total.

As an adult, I've drank roughly: _____ alcoholic drinks in total.

As an adult, I've smoked roughly: _____ joints (or blunts, bowls, or bongs) in total.

I've done about: _____ pounds of drugs.

In conclusion, I am: _____ going to hell.

Congratulations! You finished this chapter.

Now comes the fun part—figure out how much you've changed.
Are you proof that good things always stay the same, like Betty White?
Or are you proof of the power of transformation, like David Bowie?

CALCULATE YOUR SCORE!

Total all your Change-O-Meter
scores from this chapter

The number of questions
in this chapter

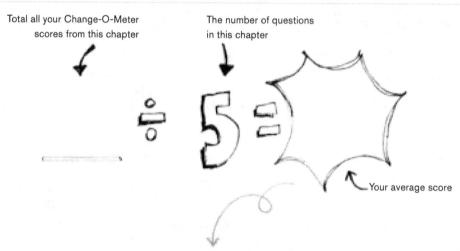

Your average score

ARE YOU A BETTY OR A BOWIE?
CIRCLE WHERE YOU FALL ON THE SPECTRUM BELOW

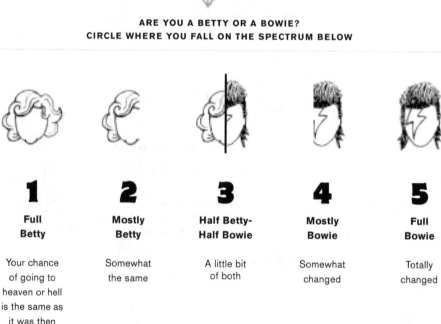

1	**2**	**3**	**4**	**5**
Full Betty	**Mostly Betty**	**Half Betty- Half Bowie**	**Mostly Bowie**	**Full Bowie**
Your chance of going to heaven or hell is the same as it was then	Somewhat the same	A little bit of both	Somewhat changed	Totally changed

What parts of your tendency to misbehave have changed the least? Did that surprise you?

What parts of your tendency to misbehave have changed the most? Did that surprise you?

What questions were the hardest to answer in this chapter and why?

Was it harder to answer about your childhood or adulthood for this chapter?

What judgments do you have, if any, on the ways you have (and have not) changed?

Do any of these results inspire you to want to change some aspect of your life? If so, what?

Final Summary

Woo-hoo! You made it to the end of this journal. Given what you wrote about your ambition in an earlier chapter, we knew you could do it. Although given what you wrote about your vices in another chapter, we thought you might just grab a bag of Doritos and call it a day. Now, for the moment you've been waiting for: How much have you changed, overall? Does it match the score you predicted in the introduction?

CALCULATE YOUR FINAL SCORE!

Total all your Change-O-Meter scores from each chapter

The number of chapters in this book

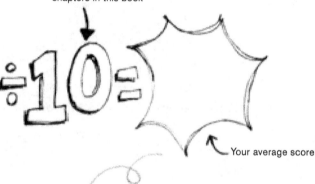

Your average score

CIRCLE YOUR FINAL SCORE HERE

1	2	3	4	5
Full Betty	**Mostly Betty**	**Half Betty-Half Bowie**	**Mostly Bowie**	**Full Bowie**
Good things never change, including you.	Somewhat the same.	A little bit of both.	Somewhat changed.	Change is good and you're living proof.

Did your score surprise you?
How do you feel about seeing your final rating?

Did your final score match your prediction from the intro of this journal?

What aspects of your life overall have changed
the least? Did that surprise you?

What aspects of your life overall have changed
the most? Did that surprise you?

What questions were the hardest to answer in this book and why?

Was it harder to answer about your childhood or adulthood in this book?

What judgments do you have, if any, on the ways
you have (and have not) changed?

Do any of these results inspire you to want to change
some aspect of your life? If so, what?

Would your teenage self have completed this journal?
How much of this journal did you complete? (No judgments.)

EXTRA CREDIT

How would your friends fare in this journal?
List 3 friends and predict what their scores
would be. Who's Betty? Who's Bowie?

Share the Shame

Want more *Mortified*? Discover the world of *Mortified* books, films, podcast, TV, stage shows, and beyond at **getmortified.com**.

Other Titles Available from Mortified:

Mortified: Real World, Real People, Real Pathetic (book)

Mortified: Love is a Battlefield (book)

Mortified Nation (home video)

The Mortified Sessions (home video)

The Mortified Guide (home video)

The Mortified Podcast (audio)

About the Authors

David Nadelberg is a writer, producer, interviewer, and public speaker. He is best known as the founder of *Mortified*, an art and media collaboration that celebrates the angst and awkwardness of growing up. His work with *Mortified* has been covered by *All Things Considered*, *This American Life*, *Boston Globe*, *Time*, and *Newsweek*, which hailed the project "a cultural phenomenon." In 2011, Nadelberg hosted two seasons of the Sundance TV interview series, *The Mortified Sessions*. He currently lives in Los Angeles where he once met the guy who played Chainsaw in *Summer School* while in line at Koo Koo Roo and is still psyched about that.

Sam Kaplan is an author and therapist living in Oakland, California. Growing up, his favorite breakfast food was Eggos, his main form of exercise was soccer, and his spirit animal (according to his friends) was a donkey. Today, his favorite breakfast food is green smoothies, his main form of exercise is typing, and his spirit animal (according to his friends) is still a donkey.

Co-Conspirator and Sounding Boards

Co-Conspirator: Neil Katcher

Sounding Boards: Joy Tutela, Robbie Simon, Pierce Purselley, Leonard Hyman, Hadley Dion, Cyrina Fiallo, Katy May Spencer, Eliza Swords, Mike Mayer, Mike Stern, Lance Roberts, Radiotopia, and the entire *Mortified* community.

CPSIA information can be obtained
at www.ICGtesting.com
Printed in the USA
JSHW030511270121
11254JS00001B/5